A PERSONAL GUIDE TO GETTING
INTENTIONAL RESULTS

REIGNITE YOUR *Why*

DR. BLAIR

innovation

commitment

This productivity planner belongs to

_____

Start date

_____

passion

accountability

REIGNITE YOUR WHY

Copyright © 2022 Dr. Blair
All rights reserved.

No part of this book may be reproduced, distributed or transmitted in any form by any means, graphic, electronic, or mechanical, including photocopy, recording, taping, or by any information storage or retrieval system, without permission in writing from the publisher, except in the case of reprints in the context of reviews, quotes, or references.

Unless otherwise indicated, scripture quotations are from the Holy Bible, King James Version.

All rights reserved.

To all the women who are ready to reignite your "why" and unlock your potential, may this book serve as a tool to move you forward along your journey.

Consider each day a new opportunity.

GREETINGS!

Congratulations on taking the initial steps in your journey of personal self-discovery. Now is a great time to unlock your potential. I am delighted that you have selected the *Reignite Your Why* planner to organize your thoughts, schedule your personal endeavors, and reevaluate your perspective. As you embark on this journey over the next twelve months, I encourage you to be open-minded and engaged as you enter into another year. Consider each day a new opportunity and stay open to the newness and fresh perspective offered to you through the gift of a new day. Before moving forward with this planner, take a deep breath and say to yourself, "This is the time to begin establishing, creating, and starting something new."

This productivity planner, packed with monthly lessons that are geared toward reigniting your "why" and engaging your thinking, is written in a personal, reflective dialogue that inspires thought and creativity. As you plan and organize the next twelve months of your journey, adopt an intentional approach. Take the time to get to know yourself. Each month includes teachings designed to help you learn strategies intended to create a vision, reflect on your strengths, and clarify areas for growth to ultimately create your schedule with your personal goals in mind.

I wish you increased success and a reflective and authentic year that represents your personal growth and self-discovery.

Happy planning,

Dr. Blair

TABLE OF CONTENTS

How to Use This Planner 8

Resilience 11

Affirmations 12

Looking Back—With the Purpose of Moving Forward 13

Month 1: Establish Goals for New Beginnings 15

Month 2: Create Your Vision 33

Month 3: Manage Your Priorities and Distractions 53

Month 4: Purposefully Schedule Your Time 71

Month 5: Create Boundaries 87

Month 6: Mid-Year Checkpoint 105

Month 7: Learn to Be Good to Yourself 123

Month 8: Unlock Your Potential 141

Month 9: Focus Your Thinking 159

Month 10: Release Your Fears 177

Month 11: Find the Right Balance 195

Month 12: End-of-Year Assessment 213

HOW TO USE THIS PLANNER

Reignite Your Why is designed to use for one year and includes twelve sections with a monthly overview. One of the unique aspects of this planner is that it is **not dated**. Therefore, you have the flexibility to begin planning during any month of the year. The monthly layout is designed to encourage you to reevaluate your thoughts and actions and remain on track in achieving your personal goals. Throughout this planner, you will find various sections that will evoke your thought patterns and encourage you to be more intentional about your planning. Each section is designed to challenge your perspective, spark your growth, and help you achieve your goals. The sections below provide an overview of each section and how to use it:

Monthly Discovery: There are twelve discovery sections—one for each month of the year. At the beginning of each month is a short lesson on a different topic that will promote growth in one specific aspect of your life. This section will introduce a new topic and encourage you to reevaluate where you land in this area.

Take Action: This section acts as a catalyst to promote change by asking you to complete a task or chart and thus put learning into practice. Each month, this section will challenge you to strengthen your learning.

Think It Over: Following the "Monthly Discovery" lesson and "Take Action" challenge, you will find a reflection section where you can apply what you have learned and incorporate these lessons into your weekly and monthly goals.

Monthly Calendar: The monthly calendar provides a space for you to track and view your planned activities and events for the entire month. Keep your calendar up to date throughout the month to stay on task and plan your time intentionally.

Monthly Goals: Use this section to reflect on the overall goals you want to accomplish for the month. List them in this section as a reflective reference.

Weekly Outlook: In this section, keep your monthly goals in mind by creating your weekly schedule and outlining what you want to accomplish each week. Give thought to how you can achieve the monthly goals you set by creating action items and using the task boxes to check off completed items. This process will help you stay motivated and on track.

Monthly Reflection: In this section, you will complete a personal review of the month and respond to questions that will help you assess your productivity while reflecting on areas requiring improvement. The questions you will reflect on and answer for each month are as follows:

- Which goals did you complete this month?
- What was your favorite moment this month?
- Who or what kept you motivated this month?
- What is something positive from this month that you can bring into next month?

Whether you are a thoughtful organizer or you struggle to organize with intention, this planner is for you. Use it as a step-by-step guide as you grow throughout the year!

action

reflection

discovery

goals

RESILIENCE

The process used to begin something new and remain consistent takes resilience. The purpose of this planner is to motivate you toward greater productivity.

While working through the planner, keep in mind the following 5-step module:

1. Realize that you play an active role in your productivity.
2. Engage regularly. Plan to work through each month and apply these principles to your daily life.
3. This planner is intentionally non-dated. Start and continue at your own pace.
4. Focus on steps you need to take and work toward your goal.
5. Celebrate your wins throughout your year.

The next page contains positive affirmation statements designed to keep you inspired and motivated. You are encouraged to read each statement aloud, absorb the positivity, and embody the statements. During your journey throughout the year, refer back to these statements for inspiration and encouragement. Each week, you will have an opportunity to create and add your own affirmation in the "Weekly Outlook" section to keep you motivated.

I am enough!

Today will be a great day!

I have the power to create change!

My possibilities are endless!

I am in control of my thoughts, feelings, and choices!

I am beautiful!

I am doing my best!

I am brave!

I can achieve anything I set my mind to!

I will be present in every moment!

My dreams are possible!

I am confident!

I am fearless!

I can do this!

LOOKING BACK—WITH THE PURPOSE OF MOVING FORWARD

Before you embark on something new, take time to reflect on your *past* experiences. Dedicate some time to read and reflect on the following questions in this section.

Use this initial part of your journey to explore changes you would like to make or enhance and set intentions for how you will use this planner. Gain an understanding of anything preventing you from achieving your goals. Go a step further and take into consideration which improvements you need to make to move forward.

Reflection Questions:

1. What did you learn about yourself over the past twelve months?

2. What is out of focus in your life?

3. What prevents you from focusing?

4. If you could change one thing right now, what would it be?

5. What are three excuses you often make?

6. Which distractions can you eliminate?

7. What do you feel you need more of in your life?

MONTH 1

ESTABLISH GOALS FOR NEW BEGINNINGS

*The start of something new begins
with a renewed perspective.*

MONTHLY DISCOVERY

Whether you are starting this journey at the beginning of the year in January or mid-year in June, the good news is that there is never a bad time to start fresh. With your endgame in mind, let's begin by establishing goals. Setting goals will help you create a plan and remain focused throughout this process, serving as a road map that can lead you on a personal journey to live purposefully.

When you set goals, commit to writing them down and planning steps to accomplish them. Begin by carefully considering what you would like to achieve, knowing your goals should align with your top priorities to maximize the possibility of success. Goals should be motivational and valuable. Before you begin to create your goals, reflect on the "Looking Back—With the Purpose of Moving Forward" section.

Take some time to reflect on your responses to the questions. When writing down your goals, complete the following three steps to ensure each goal is valuable to your progress:

- Provide specific details
- Measure and monitor your progress
- Set a date of completion

Complete the "Take Action" section below and make a personal decision to live intentionally this year and thus unlock your potential.

TAKE ACTION

Begin your journey by creating your personal goals! In this section, scale your goals to "big-picture" thinking. As you work through the planner, you will have an opportunity to break down your big-picture goals into weekly goals each month. Please see the provided examples and use the space below to write your goals.

Examples of Big Picture Goals:

My goal is to <u>grow my coaching practice</u> by <u>fifteen clients</u> by <u>December 31,   </u>. This goal is important because <u>I want to help women leaders find success in achieving their personal endeavors.</u>

My goal is to <u>increase my knowledge in the area of leadership</u> by <u>reading five leadership books by December 31,   </u>. This goal is important because <u>I want to learn more about the requirements of leadership prior to applying for a leadership position.</u>

Formula: My goal is to (provide specific details) ....

....

by (measurable to monitor progress) ....

by (date of completion) ....

This goal is important because: ....

....

Formula: My goal is to (provide specific details) ....

....

by (measurable to monitor progress) ....

by (date of completion) ....

This goal is important because: ....

....

Formula: My goal is to (provide specific details) ....

....

by (measurable to monitor progress) ....

by (date of completion) ....

This goal is important because: ....

....

THINK IT OVER

Which activities do I need to eliminate to reach my goals?

MONTHLY CALENDAR

SUNDAY	MONDAY	TUESDAY	WEDNESDAY

THURSDAY	FRIDAY	SATURDAY

Monthly Goals

1. ....
2. ....
3. ....
4. ....
5. ....

Friendly Reminders

1. ....
2. ....
3. ....
4. ....
5. ....

WEEKLY OUTLOOK

Date	MONDAY Action Items	Status	Date	TUESDAY Action Items	Status	Date	WEDNESDAY Action Items	Status

Top 3 goals for this week:

1.

2.

3.

Your future is created by what you do today, not tomorrow. —Anonymous

THURSDAY		
Date	Action Items	Status

FRIDAY		
Date	Action Items	Status

SATURDAY/SUNDAY		
Date	Action Items	Status

Today I am grateful for: ....

....

Weekly affirmation: ....

....

WEEKLY OUTLOOK

MONDAY			TUESDAY			WEDNESDAY		
Date	Action Items	Status	Date	Action Items	Status	Date	Action Items	Status

Top 3 goals for this week:

1. ....

2. ....

3. ....

Make a personal decision that you will live intentionally this year and unlock your potential.

THURSDAY			FRIDAY			SATURDAY/SUNDAY		
Date	Action Items	Status	Date	Action Items	Status	Date	Action Items	Status

Today I am grateful for: ....

....

Weekly affirmation: ....

....

WEEKLY OUTLOOK

Date	MONDAY Action Items	Status	Date	TUESDAY Action Items	Status	Date	WEDNESDAY Action Items	Status

Top 3 goals for this week:

1. ....

2. ....

3. ....

Make plans for your new goals. And press towards achieving the goals with all your strength. —Lailah Gifty Akita

THURSDAY			FRIDAY			SATURDAY/SUNDAY		
Date	Action Items	Status	Date	Action Items	Status	Date	Action Items	Status

Today I am grateful for: ....

....

Weekly affirmation: ....

....

WEEKLY OUTLOOK

Date	MONDAY Action Items	Status

Date	TUESDAY Action Items	Status

Date	WEDNESDAY Action Items	Status

Top 3 goals for this week:

1. ....

2. ....

3. ....

Goals serve as a road map that can lead you on a personal journey to live purposefully.

Date	THURSDAY Action Items	Status	Date	FRIDAY Action Items	Status	Date	SATURDAY/SUNDAY Action Items	Status

Today I am grateful for: ....

....

Weekly affirmation: ....

....

 MONTHLY REFLECTION

Take an opportunity to review the month.

Which goals did you complete this month?

....

....

....

What was your favorite moment this month?

....

....

....

Who or what kept you motivated this month?

....

....

....

What is something positive from this month that you can bring into the next month?

....

....

....

NOTES

NOTES

(MONTH 2)

CREATE YOUR VISION

Where there is no vision, the people perish.

—Proverbs 29:18

MONTHLY DISCOVERY

Creating your vision will require you to focus, exert effort intentionally, and practice efficiency. Remember that you are the author of your vision, so take the necessary steps to produce the vision you want to see. A vision board is a visual representation of everything you want to have, be, or do in your life. Creating a board that outlines personal aspirations is often a rewarding adventure. It provides an opportunity for you to brainstorm what you would like to accomplish and a space to compile your ideas. Moreover, it provides a blueprint approach that meshes all of your ideas together and serves as a reminder throughout the year for all goals you want to accomplish.

When creating your vision board, schedule time to think through your personal strengths. Consider how you can leverage these to work toward organizing your vision and goals. This activity should be deliberate and completed within a set time frame. Use the following model to aid in the personalization of your vision board:

V – Visualize a theme for your board

I – Identify everything you want to accomplish within the next year

S – Schedule a set time frame to brainstorm your goals

I – Intentionally organize your goals into categories

O – Observe your categories and determine how your strengths can add value to your goals

N – Navigate your categories and create your vision board in a way that aligns in a meaningful way

TAKE ACTION

This month, you are challenged to create your personal vision board. Use this activity to embrace a new perspective and gain a fresh outlook on new possibilities.

Here are some suggestions for creating your vision board:

1. Gather materials (glue stick, scissors, markers, poster board).
2. Think about which categories (e.g., family, relationships, education) you would like your board to focus on.
3. Gain clarity on what you've accomplished, brainstorming on how to build on your past success.
4. Open your mind to different areas you may want to see change in.
5. Select visuals, words, or phrases (via magazines, photos, images) that represent goals you have brainstormed.
6. Add the visuals, words, and phrases to your board along with any embellishments that feel right to you.

CREATE YOUR

VISION BOARD

THINK IT OVER

Take a moment to think through the completion of your vision board. Now that you have a concrete visual representation of your goals, how can you utilize the board to help reach them?

NOTES

MONTHLY CALENDAR

SUNDAY	MONDAY	TUESDAY	WEDNESDAY

THURSDAY	FRIDAY	SATURDAY

Monthly Goals

1. ......
2. ......
3. ......
4. ......
5. ......

Friendly Reminders

1. ......
2. ......
3. ......
4. ......
5. ......

WEEKLY OUTLOOK

Date	MONDAY Action Items	Status	Date	TUESDAY Action Items	Status	Date	WEDNESDAY Action Items	Status

Top 3 goals for this week:

1. ....

2. ....

3. ....

Creating a vision requires focus, effort, and efficiency.

Date	THURSDAY Action Items	Status	Date	FRIDAY Action Items	Status	Date	SATURDAY/SUNDAY Action Items	Status

Today I am grateful for: ....

....

Weekly affirmation: ....

....

WEEKLY OUTLOOK

MONDAY			TUESDAY			WEDNESDAY		
Date	Action Items	Status	Date	Action Items	Status	Date	Action Items	Status

Top 3 goals for this week:

1. ....

2. ....

3. ....

Dissatisfaction and discouragement are not caused by the absence of things but the absence of vision. —Anonymous

THURSDAY			FRIDAY			SATURDAY/SUNDAY		
Date	Action Items	Status	Date	Action Items	Status	Date	Action Items	Status

Today I am grateful for: ....

....

Weekly affirmation: ....

....

WEEKLY OUTLOOK

MONDAY		
Date	Action Items	Status

TUESDAY		
Date	Action Items	Status

WEDNESDAY		
Date	Action Items	Status

Top 3 goals for this week:

1. ....

2. ....

3. ....

> *If you don't like something, change it. If you can't change it, change your attitude.* —Maya Angelou

THURSDAY			FRIDAY			SATURDAY/SUNDAY		
Date	Action Items	Status	Date	Action Items	Status	Date	Action Items	Status

Today I am grateful for: ....

....

Weekly affirmation: ....

....

WEEKLY OUTLOOK

Date	MONDAY Action Items	Status	Date	TUESDAY Action Items	Status	Date	WEDNESDAY Action Items	Status

Top 3 goals for this week:

1. ....

2. ....

3. ....

Make your vision so clear that your fears become irrelevant. —Anonymous

Date	THURSDAY Action Items	Status	Date	FRIDAY Action Items	Status	Date	SATURDAY/SUNDAY Action Items	Status

Today I am grateful for: ....

....

Weekly affirmation: ....

....

MONTHLY REFLECTION

Take an opportunity to review the month.

Which goals did you complete this month?

....
....
....

What was your favorite moment this month?

....
....
....

Who or what kept you motivated this month?

....
....
....

What is something positive from this month that you can bring into the next month?

....
....
....

NOTES

NOTES

Month 3

MANAGE YOUR PRIORITIES AND DISTRACTIONS

Living your purpose is not only what you're here for, but it also empowers you to succeed.

—Valorie Burton

MONTHLY DISCOVERY

Are you making the best use of your time? Accomplishing your goals is an intentional practice. How often have you thought to yourself, I don't feel like I have accomplished anything at the end of a busy day? Managing the hours in your day is one key component needed to accomplish your goals. One way to manage your priorities is to create a schedule: an outline that adds value to your daily routine and provides a blueprint of each hour of each day. Learning to schedule your activities throughout the day can help you be more mindful of what you would like to achieve.

Distractions are things that deter or prevent us from giving our full attention to completing scheduled priorities that lead to the completion of our overall goals. These daily unexpected interruptions steal our attention away from priorities and result in less productivity. Some examples include responding to unexpected text messages, scrolling through social media for long periods of time, or taking an unscheduled phone call.

Scheduling can help you maximize your efforts to complete your goals and eliminate many distractions. Whether this occurs at the beginning or end of the week, create a routine for scheduling your time each day. Identify how much time you want to spend on personal endeavors and professional priorities, and attempt to establish a balance between both. Use the following four-step strategy to create your schedule:

1. **Take time to ponder.** Before planning your schedule, spend time thinking about what you would like to accomplish throughout the day and week ahead. Be creative and decide how much time you would like to dedicate to each action item.

2. **Create a to-do list.** Review your planned personal goals and make a list of actionable items.

3. **Determine which tasks are a priority and which are nonessential.** Identify which action items are priorities—"must do" items—and which are nonessential, meaning you can complete them at a later time.

4. **Analyze and review.** Review your schedule. Do you have any discretionary time? If you need to make adjustments, identify action items you can delegate to others or shift to another time.

TAKE ACTION

Based on what you know about your schedule, outline how you will use your time over the next 48 hours. Use the chart below to create a snapshot of commitments, considering items such as sleep, meals, exercise, work, family time, volunteering, and activities.

Time	Day 1	Day 2
5:00 am		
6:00 am		
7:00 am		
8:00 am		
9:00 am		
10:00 am		
11:00 am		
12:00 pm		
1:00 pm		
2:00 pm		
3:00 pm		
4:00 pm		
5:00 pm		
6:00 pm		
7:00 pm		
8:00 pm		
9:00 pm		
10:00 pm		
11:00 pm		
12:00 am		
1:00 am		
2:00 am		
3:00 am		
4:00 am		

THINK IT OVER

Are you satisfied with how you scheduled the past **48** hours? Explain.

What improvements (if any) can you make to your schedule?

NOTES

MONTHLY CALENDAR

SUNDAY	MONDAY	TUESDAY	WEDNESDAY

THURSDAY	FRIDAY	SATURDAY

Monthly Goals

1. ....
2. ....
3. ....
4. ....
5. ....

Friendly Reminders

1. ....
2. ....
3. ....
4. ....
5. ....

WEEKLY OUTLOOK

MONDAY			TUESDAY			WEDNESDAY		
Date	Action Items	Status	Date	Action Items	Status	Date	Action Items	Status

Top 3 goals for this week:

1. ....

2. ....

3. ....

The key is not to prioritize what's on your schedule, but to schedule your priorities. —Stephen R. Covey

Date	THURSDAY Action Items	Status

Date	FRIDAY Action Items	Status

Date	SATURDAY/SUNDAY Action Items	Status

Today I am grateful for: ....

....

Weekly affirmation: ....

....

WEEKLY OUTLOOK

MONDAY			TUESDAY			WEDNESDAY		
Date	Action Items	Status	Date	Action Items	Status	Date	Action Items	Status

Top 3 goals for this week:

1. ....

2. ....

3. ....

Learning to schedule your priorities is an essential ingredient to remaining focused on building personal resilience.

THURSDAY			FRIDAY			SATURDAY/SUNDAY		
Date	Action Items	Status	Date	Action Items	Status	Date	Action Items	Status

Today I am grateful for: ....

....

Weekly affirmation: ....

....

WEEKLY OUTLOOK

Date	MONDAY Action Items	Status

Date	TUESDAY Action Items	Status

Date	WEDNESDAY Action Items	Status

Top 3 goals for this week:

1. ....

2. ....

3. ....

The key to success is to focus on goals, not obstacles. —Unknown

Date	THURSDAY Action Items	Status	Date	FRIDAY Action Items	Status	Date	SATURDAY/SUNDAY Action Items	Status

Today I am grateful for: ....

....

Weekly affirmation: ....

....

WEEKLY OUTLOOK

Date	MONDAY Action Items	Status	Date	TUESDAY Action Items	Status	Date	WEDNESDAY Action Items	Status

Top 3 goals for this week:

1. ....

2. ....

3. ....

A woman who lives with the stress of an overwhelmed schedule will often ache with the sadness of an underwhelmed soul. —Lysa TerKeurst

Date	THURSDAY Action Items	Status

Date	FRIDAY Action Items	Status

Date	SATURDAY/SUNDAY Action Items	Status

Today I am grateful for: ....

....

Weekly affirmation: ....

....

MONTHLY REFLECTION

Take an opportunity to review the month.

Which goals did you complete this month?

What was your favorite moment this month?

Who or what kept you motivated this month?

What is something positive from this month that you can bring into the next month?

NOTES

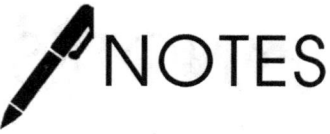 NOTES

MONTH 4

PURPOSEFULLY SCHEDULE YOUR TIME

*The decisions you make determine the schedule you keep.
The schedule you keep determines the life that you live.
And how you live your life
determines how you spend your soul.*

—Lysa TerKeurst

MONTHLY DISCOVERY

Time is one of the most precious resources we have. Many people believe time can be managed. Although each individual is offered the same amount of time in a day, I often hear individuals converse about not having enough time. They say statements like, "If I only had more time in a day," "One day I hope to have enough time to . . . ," or "I'll consider this once I have more time." Practice making the best use of your time to ensure you add value to your purpose and goals and work intentionally toward achieving them. Managing your priorities will help you use the time you have wisely each day.

24 hours/day = 1,440 minutes = 86,400 seconds

The truth of the matter is: you will never have more time in a day than stated above. Are you *scheduling* your time? You may ask yourself, *Why* should I schedule my time? A schedule detailing how you will spend your time each day determines the importance of goals and activities you need and want to accomplish. Scheduling time also helps you overcome distractions that interrupt time designated for specific tasks. After all, we can't do everything and do it well at the same time.

TAKE ACTION

The challenge for this month is to take an honest assessment of the roles you play in life and how effectively you use your time. Take a moment to complete the following prompts.

What are the top 5 roles (e.g., mother, wife, aunt, caretaker, friend) you fulfill in your life?

1. ....
2. ....
3. ....
4. ....
5. ....

Identify 3 to 5 distractions (e.g., watching TV, surfing the internet) that cause you to use your time unwisely.

1. ....
2. ....
3. ....
4. ....
5. ....

MONTHLY CALENDAR

SUNDAY	MONDAY	TUESDAY	WEDNESDAY

THURSDAY	FRIDAY	SATURDAY

Monthly Goals

1. ....
2. ....
3. ....
4. ....
5. ....

Friendly Reminders

1. ....
2. ....
3. ....
4. ....
5. ....

WEEKLY OUTLOOK

MONDAY			TUESDAY			WEDNESDAY		
Date	Action Items	Status	Date	Action Items	Status	Date	Action Items	Status

Top 3 goals for this week:

1. ....

2. ....

3. ....

Manage your distractions and schedule your time to ensure you make the most out of each day.

THURSDAY			FRIDAY			SATURDAY/SUNDAY		
Date	Action Items	Status	Date	Action Items	Status	Date	Action Items	Status

Today I am grateful for: ....

....

Weekly affirmation: ....

....

WEEKLY OUTLOOK

MONDAY				TUESDAY				WEDNESDAY		
Date	Action Items	Status		Date	Action Items	Status		Date	Action Items	Status

Top 3 goals for this week:

1. ....

2. ....

3. ....

Practice making the best use of your time to ensure that you add value to your purpose and goals and then work intentionally toward achieving them.

THURSDAY			FRIDAY			SATURDAY/SUNDAY		
Date	Action Items	Status	Date	Action Items	Status	Date	Action Items	Status

Today I am grateful for: ....

....

Weekly affirmation: ....

....

WEEKLY OUTLOOK

Date	MONDAY Action Items	Status

Date	TUESDAY Action Items	Status

Date	WEDNESDAY Action Items	Status

Top 3 goals for this week:

1. ....

2. ....

3. ....

A daily schedule for how you will spend your time determines the importance of goals and activities you want or need to accomplish.

THURSDAY				FRIDAY				SATURDAY/SUNDAY		
Date	Action Items	Status		Date	Action Items	Status		Date	Action Items	Status

Today I am grateful for: ....

....

Weekly affirmation: ....

....

WEEKLY OUTLOOK

Date	MONDAY Action Items	Status	Date	TUESDAY Action Items	Status	Date	WEDNESDAY Action Items	Status

Top 3 goals for this week:

1. ....

2. ....

3. ....

Most of us spend too much time on what is urgent and not enough time on what is important. —Stephen R. Covey

THURSDAY			FRIDAY			SATURDAY/SUNDAY		
Date	Action Items	Status	Date	Action Items	Status	Date	Action Items	Status

Today I am grateful for: ....

....

Weekly affirmation: ....

....

 MONTHLY REFLECTION

Take an opportunity to review the month.

Which goals did you complete this month?

....
....
....

What was your favorite moment this month?

....
....
....

Who or what kept you motivated this month?

....
....
....

What is something positive from this month that you can bring into the next month?

....
....
....

NOTES

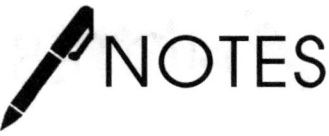

NOTES

Month 5

CREATE BOUNDARIES

Boundaries define us. They define what is me and is not me. A boundary shows me where I end and someone else begins, leading me to a sense of ownership.
Knowing what I am to own and take responsibility for gives me freedom.

—Henry Cloud

MONTHLY DISCOVERY

Achieving goals takes intentional planning and preparation. If you are serious about achieving your goals and creating the space required to manage your distractions using a healthy approach, there is a need to establish boundaries. Dictionary.com describes the word "boundary" as "a line that marks the limit." If you will be more intentional about achieving your goals this year, it is important to give some thought to setting limits in your life.

Before we discuss the characteristics of boundaries, take some time to reflect on the list of roles you created in the "Manage Your Priorities" and "Distractions" sections of this planner. The roles we play can deter us from focusing on our own personal needs, goals, and purpose. On a consistent basis, we say "yes" and "no" without considering how our decision impacts our personal pursuits. Establishing boundaries gives us an opportunity to decide what we have the capacity to take on and fulfill. Boundaries are personally created terms and conditions that allow us to take ownership of the decision-making process and engage our perspective to move forward with our purpose in mind.

The first step in establishing boundaries is to make better use of the words "yes" and "no" rather than merely using them without giving thought to how the response will impact the goals and activities surrounding our future priorities. Establishing boundaries helps us act with more purpose and not rush. Think about how often you respond to daily requests or demands without considering the impact it will have on your life. We often respond with an affirming "yes" to invitations or requests because we don't want to hurt others' feelings. Likewise, we may feel awkward if we use the word "no" because we're overly concerned about how the other person will view us after hearing the response. It's important to remember that when you say yes to a request or invitation, you are also saying no to something else. For example, if you are trying to adopt a healthier lifestyle, you may need to reconsider saying yes to lunch in the office break room that is usually stocked with cookies and pastries. If you are planning to buy a home, you may have to say no to purchases made outside of a planned budget. If you're seeking a promotion at work, you may want to consider taking on an extra project outside of your assigned work responsibilities. Before you rush to make a decision, be sure to carefully consider the trade of your yes or no response and the impact it will have. Are you willing to say yes or no to something that will impact whether you achieve your personal goals?

The decisions you make throughout the day matter, and no decision is an isolated choice. Be observant and intentional about how you use the days, hours, and minutes of this month. Consider your established goals and where your decisions will take you.

TAKE ACTION

This month's challenge is to establish boundaries as you make decisions. Prior to making decisions this month, use the following guiding questions in the chart below to help you during your decision-making process.

1. Have you considered what is being asked of you?

   ....

   ....

   ....

2. Do you have the capacity to complete this obligation or request?

   ....

   ....

   ....

3. Will this request distract you from completing your goals?

   ....

   ....

   ....

4. What kind of attitude do you have regarding this request?

   ....

   ....

   ....

THINK IT OVER

1. List two situations where you need to establish boundaries.

2. Briefly identify how you will set boundaries for the situations listed above.

MONTHLY CALENDAR

SUNDAY	MONDAY	TUESDAY	WEDNESDAY

THURSDAY	FRIDAY	SATURDAY

Monthly Goals

1. ....
2. ....
3. ....
4. ....
5. ....

Friendly Reminders

1. ....
2. ....
3. ....
4. ....
5. ....

WEEKLY OUTLOOK

MONDAY				TUESDAY				WEDNESDAY		
Date	Action Items	Status		Date	Action Items	Status		Date	Action Items	Status

Top 3 goals for this week:

1. ....

2. ....

3. ....

If you will be more intentional about achieving your goals this year, it is important to give some thought to which areas of your life will benefit from limits.

THURSDAY			FRIDAY			SATURDAY/SUNDAY		
Date	Action Items	Status	Date	Action Items	Status	Date	Action Items	Status

Today I am grateful for: ....

....

Weekly affirmation: ....

....

WEEKLY OUTLOOK

Date	MONDAY Action Items	Status

Date	TUESDAY Action Items	Status

Date	WEDNESDAY Action Items	Status

Top 3 goals for this week:

1. ....

2. ....

3. ....

The decisions you make through the day matter, and no decision is an isolated choice.

THURSDAY			FRIDAY			SATURDAY/SUNDAY		
Date	Action Items	Status	Date	Action Items	Status	Date	Action Items	Status

Today I am grateful for: ....

....

Weekly affirmation: ....

....

WEEKLY OUTLOOK

MONDAY		
Date	Action Items	Status

TUESDAY		
Date	Action Items	Status

WEDNESDAY		
Date	Action Items	Status

Top 3 goals for this week:

1. ....

2. ....

3. ....

> *When we fail to set boundaries and hold people accountable, we feel used and mistreated.* —Brené Brown

Date	THURSDAY Action Items	Status	Date	FRIDAY Action Items	Status	Date	SATURDAY/SUNDAY Action Items	Status

Today I am grateful for: ....

....

Weekly affirmation: ....

....

🔍 WEEKLY OUTLOOK

Date	MONDAY Action Items	Status		Date	TUESDAY Action Items	Status		Date	WEDNESDAY Action Items	Status

Top 3 goals for this week:

1. ....

2. ....

3. ....

Boundaries are part of self-care. They are healthy, normal, and necessary.
—Doreen Virtue

THURSDAY			FRIDAY			SATURDAY/SUNDAY		
Date	Action Items	Status	Date	Action Items	Status	Date	Action Items	Status

Today I am grateful for: ....

....

Weekly affirmation: ....

....

MONTHLY REFLECTION

Take an opportunity to review the month.

Which goals did you complete this month?

....

....

....

What was your favorite moment this month?

....

....

....

Who or what kept you motivated this month?

....

....

....

What is something positive from this month that you can bring into the next month?

....

....

....

NOTES

# NOTES

MONTH 6

MID-YEAR CHECKPOINT

The only limit to the height of your achievements is the reach of your dreams and your willingness to work for them.

—Michelle Obama

MONTHLY DISCOVERY

Congratulations!

You have reached the midpoint in your journey. The challenge for this month is to take an active assessment of where you are. Spend some time reflecting on everything you have accomplished and assess areas ripe for reevaluation.

Think about the progress you have made since beginning your journey with this productivity planner. Which goals have you achieved? Which daily practices have you incorporated? What worked during the past months, and where do you need to make improvements? Perhaps your goals planned at the beginning of the year are now fulfilled. Consider setting new goals, diving deeper into what you would like to accomplish.

This is also the time to celebrate your wins. Sometimes, we work so hard to reach our goals that we don't take time to reflect on our milestones and wins—both big and small. After all, the wins are what led us to form consistent habits and keep track of our progress.

TAKE ACTION

Review the goals you set in the "Establish Goals for New Beginnings" section. Reevaluate each goal by reflecting on the following questions:

1. How are you moving toward achieving your big-picture goal(s)?

2. What keeps you motivated?

3. What brings you the most peace and balance in life?

4. Where are you not putting enough energy?

5. Where are you putting too much energy?

Perhaps you have approached this section and would like to create new goals. Let me reassure you that it is not too late! Use the formula below to create additional goals for the remainder of the year.

Formula: My goal is to (provide specific details) ....

....

by (measurable to monitor progress) ....

by (date of completion) ....

This goal is important because: ....

....

Formula: My goal is to (provide specific details) ....

....

by (measurable to monitor progress) ....

by (date of completion) ....

This goal is important because: ....

....

Formula: My goal is to (provide specific details) ....

....

by (measurable to monitor progress) ....

by (date of completion) ....

This goal is important because: ....

....

THINK IT OVER

1. What are some limiting beliefs that might be holding you back from achieving your goals?

2. What are 5 ways you can get out of your comfort zone for the remainder of the year?

MONTHLY CALENDAR

SUNDAY	MONDAY	TUESDAY	WEDNESDAY

THURSDAY	FRIDAY	SATURDAY

Monthly Goals

1. ....
2. ....
3. ....
4. ....
5. ....

Friendly Reminders

1. ....
2. ....
3. ....
4. ....
5. ....

🔍 WEEKLY OUTLOOK

MONDAY			TUESDAY			WEDNESDAY		
Date 📅	Action Items ✈	Status ✓	Date 📅	Action Items ✈	Status ✓	Date 📅	Action Items ✈	Status ✓

Top 3 goals for this week:

1. ....

2. ....

3. ....

Getting organized in the normal routines of life and finishing little projects you've started is an important first step toward realizing larger goals. If you can't get a handle on the small things, how will you ever get it together to focus on the big things? —Joyce Meyer

THURSDAY			FRIDAY			SATURDAY/SUNDAY		
Date	Action Items	Status	Date	Action Items	Status	Date	Action Items	Status

Today I am grateful for: ....

....

Weekly affirmation: ....

....

WEEKLY OUTLOOK

MONDAY			TUESDAY			WEDNESDAY		
Date	Action Items	Status	Date	Action Items	Status	Date	Action Items	Status

Top 3 goals for this week:

1. ....

2. ....

3. ....

We hold ourselves back in ways both big and small, by lacking self-confidence, by not raising our hands, and by pulling back when we should be leaning in. —Sheryl Sandberg

THURSDAY			FRIDAY			SATURDAY/SUNDAY		
Date	Action Items	Status	Date	Action Items	Status	Date	Action Items	Status

Today I am grateful for: ....

....

Weekly affirmation: ....

....

WEEKLY OUTLOOK

MONDAY			TUESDAY			WEDNESDAY		
Date	Action Items	Status	Date	Action Items	Status	Date	Action Items	Status

Top 3 goals for this week:

1. ....

2. ....

3. ....

Goals help you channel your energy into action. —Les Brown

THURSDAY			FRIDAY			SATURDAY/SUNDAY		
Date	Action Items	Status	Date	Action Items	Status	Date	Action Items	Status

Today I am grateful for: ....

....

Weekly affirmation: ....

....

WEEKLY OUTLOOK

MONDAY			TUESDAY			WEDNESDAY		
Date	Action Items	Status	Date	Action Items	Status	Date	Action Items	Status

Top 3 goals for this week:

1. ....

2. ....

3. ....

Take time to celebrate your wins!

THURSDAY			FRIDAY			SATURDAY/SUNDAY		
Date	Action Items	Status	Date	Action Items	Status	Date	Action Items	Status

Today I am grateful for: ....

....

Weekly affirmation: ....

....

MONTHLY REFLECTION

Take an opportunity to review the month.

Which goals did you complete this month?

....
....
....

What was your favorite moment this month?

....
....
....

Who or what kept you motivated this month?

....
....
....

What is something positive from this month that you can bring into the next month?

....
....
....

NOTES

MONTH 7

LEARN TO BE GOOD TO YOURSELF

Breathe. Let go. And remind yourself that this very moment is the only one you know you have for sure.

—Oprah

MONTHLY DISCOVERY

In the Month 4 challenge, you were asked to give thought to how you schedule your time and create a schedule of your activities and events. Did you set aside a time to attend to your *personal* needs? This month, we will examine the importance of self-care. We spend so many hours helping others prioritize their needs: scheduling appointments, family gatherings, school activities, meals, volunteer activities, domestic chores, childcare, senior care, holiday events, and the list goes on and on. Self-care is important, helping us feel rejuvenated and refreshed. We are sometimes so consumed with getting things done for others that we forget to take care of ourselves. So, I'll pose the same question to you again: do you set time aside for self-care?

The "Why" Behind Self-Care

Self-care is your own personal way of saying "my needs and wants matter." This practice involves taking time to focus on yourself, forgetting about outside distractions (to-do lists, work commitments, family requests, and so on) to focus inward and assess your needs. Reflecting back on your schedule, you may think, "With everything I am responsible for, I really don't have the time to practice self-care." I want you to disengage from this way of thinking. Self-care is a gift, and it should be viewed as such. Scheduling time for self-care isn't a frivolous act—it's a necessity! When you feel your best emotionally and physically, you can better fulfill commitments.

Here are some suggestions for ways to practice self-care:

- *Take a walk/exercise*
- *Cook your favorite meal*
- *Watch your favorite TV show*
- *Read a book*
- *Engage in a hobby*
- *Take a vacation*

TAKE ACTION

Self-care does not just happen; it must be scheduled. This month's challenge is to create self-care moments and calendar appointments that force you to take the necessary actions to improve your self-care habits.

1. What is one thing you can do for yourself today to make yourself a priority?

   ....

   ....

2. Create a list of things you would do if you could carve out personal time during the week.

   1. ....

   2. ....

   3. ....

   4. ....

   5. ....

THINK IT OVER

After you complete one or more self-care activities, write down your experience here.

How did the activity affect your day?

NOTES

MONTHLY CALENDAR

SUNDAY	MONDAY	TUESDAY	WEDNESDAY

THURSDAY	FRIDAY	SATURDAY

Monthly Goals

1. ....
2. ....
3. ....
4. ....
5. ....

Friendly Reminders

1. ....
2. ....
3. ....
4. ....
5. ....

WEEKLY OUTLOOK

MONDAY		
Date	Action Items	Status

TUESDAY		
Date	Action Items	Status

WEDNESDAY		
Date	Action Items	Status

Top 3 goals for this week:

1. ....

2. ....

3. ....

Self-care is a gift, and it should be viewed as such.

THURSDAY			FRIDAY			SATURDAY/SUNDAY		
Date	Action Items	Status	Date	Action Items	Status	Date	Action Items	Status

Today I am grateful for: ....

....

Weekly affirmation: ....

....

WEEKLY OUTLOOK

Date	MONDAY Action Items	Status	Date	TUESDAY Action Items	Status	Date	WEDNESDAY Action Items	Status

Top 3 goals for this week:

1. ....

2. ....

3. ....

Self-care is your personal way of saying my needs and wants matter.

THURSDAY			FRIDAY			SATURDAY/SUNDAY		
Date	Action Items	Status	Date	Action Items	Status	Date	Action Items	Status

Today I am grateful for: ....

....

Weekly affirmation: ....

....

WEEKLY OUTLOOK

MONDAY		
Date	Action Items	Status

TUESDAY		
Date	Action Items	Status

WEDNESDAY		
Date	Action Items	Status

Top 3 goals for this week:

1. ....

2. ....

3. ....

As you grow older, you will discover that you have two hands, one for helping yourself and one for helping others. —Maya Angelou

THURSDAY			FRIDAY			SATURDAY/SUNDAY		
Date	Action Items	Status	Date	Action Items	Status	Date	Action Items	Status

Today I am grateful for: ....

....

Weekly affirmation: ....

....

🔍 WEEKLY OUTLOOK

MONDAY			TUESDAY			WEDNESDAY		
Date 📅	Action Items ✈	Status ✓	Date 📅	Action Items ✈	Status ✓	Date 📅	Action Items ✈	Status ✓

Top 3 goals for this week:

1. ....

2. ....

3. ....

Believe in yourself and create boundaries around your time; make yourself a priority, not an option.

Date	THURSDAY Action Items	Status	Date	FRIDAY Action Items	Status	Date	SATURDAY/SUNDAY Action Items	Status

Today I am grateful for: ....

....

Weekly affirmation: ....

....

MONTHLY REFLECTION

Take an opportunity to review the month.

Which goals did you complete this month?

....

....

....

What was your favorite moment this month?

....

....

....

Who or what kept you motivated this month?

....

....

....

What is something positive from this month that you can bring into the next month?

....

....

....

# NOTES

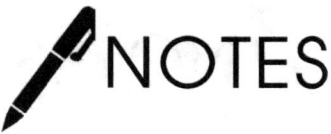 NOTES

MONTH 8

UNLOCK YOUR POTENTIAL

When preparation meets opportunity, success shows up.

MONTHLY DISCOVERY

Life is full of peaks and valleys. Unlocking your potential starts with preparation and ascertaining your inner beliefs, along with a simple phrase: **Go for it.** When you unlock your potential and give your best, nothing is impossible. What can you do today? What will you do next? How will you unlock your potential?

Here are four steps to unlocking your potential.

Step 1: Focus on your strengths. When was the last time you reflected on the things you do well? If you haven't done so lately, take some time to identify what these are. Focus on what you are good at and consider how you can use these skills to enhance your endeavors. Ask yourself questions such as, "What is working?" and "What qualifying skills do I possess?"

Step 2: Focus on your priorities. When unlocking your potential, ensure you focus on your priorities. Use your energy to concentrate on activities that will help you work toward your goals. This may require sacrificing some of your least-positive habits and unproductive relationships. Guard your calendar and be careful about what you agree to. Ensure you are aligning your schedule to meet your goals. Prior to accepting invitations or scheduling events, be sure you can fulfill commitments to the fullest. Be honest with yourself and others.

Step 3: Focus on improvement. Practice continual learning. Be on the lookout for opportunities that will allow you to learn new skills. Take advantage of resources, read self-help books, and enroll in seminars or workshops that offer skill training. Don't settle for what you already know; always find an avenue to increase your knowledge. Learn from others who are where you want to be. Observe how they do things and treat people, and gain tips on how they balance and manage. Ask questions if you don't know something. Work with other individuals in your field of choice.

Step 4: Focus on today. Whether yesterday was good or bad, realize the day is over and move forward. Try to avoid getting stuck in the past because you can't change it. Know that you can influence what happens today. Give the present day your full attention and best effort. Focusing on today will help you to strive for your highest potential, with the need to be strong and remember the higher the peak, the steeper the climb to the top. Regardless of challenging circumstances, remember to stay positive. Focus on today with intentional thoughts and actions. Rise in the morning with a purpose. Set your goals, develop your action plan, and use your time throughout the day wisely. Let go of habits that will not lead you to success and replace them with productive ones. Rely on your intuition and make choices that will lead to higher levels of productivity.

TAKE ACTION

This month, I am challenging you to think about how will unlock your potential. For each suggested step in the chart below, identify one way you can do this:

Focus on your strengths.	
Focus on your priorities.	
Focus on improvement.	
Focus on today.	

Remember, unlocking your potential begins within you. Shift your energy and use your time to close the gaps.

THINK IT OVER

Complete the following chart.

Strengths (skills/things you do well)	Areas of Improvement (skills/things you need to work on)

MONTHLY CALENDAR

SUNDAY	MONDAY	TUESDAY	WEDNESDAY

THURSDAY	FRIDAY	SATURDAY

Monthly Goals

1. ....
2. ....
3. ....
4. ....
5. ....

Friendly Reminders

1. ....
2. ....
3. ....
4. ....
5. ....

WEEKLY OUTLOOK

Date	MONDAY Action Items	Status	Date	TUESDAY Action Items	Status	Date	WEDNESDAY Action Items	Status

Top 3 goals for this week:

1. ....

2. ....

3. ....

With determination and hard work, nothing is impossible when you unlock your potential and give your best.

Date	THURSDAY Action Items	Status	Date	FRIDAY Action Items	Status	Date	SATURDAY/SUNDAY Action Items	Status

Today I am grateful for: ....

....

Weekly affirmation: ....

....

WEEKLY OUTLOOK

MONDAY		
Date	Action Items	Status

TUESDAY		
Date	Action Items	Status

WEDNESDAY		
Date	Action Items	Status

Top 3 goals for this week:

1. ....

2. ....

3. ....

One isn't necessarily born with courage, but one is born with potential. Without courage, we cannot practice any other virtue with consistency. We can't be kind, true, merciful, generous, or honest. —Maya Angelou

Date	THURSDAY Action Items	Status	Date	FRIDAY Action Items	Status	Date	SATURDAY/SUNDAY Action Items	Status

Today I am grateful for:

Weekly affirmation:

WEEKLY OUTLOOK

MONDAY				TUESDAY				WEDNESDAY		
Date	Action Items	Status		Date	Action Items	Status		Date	Action Items	Status

Top 3 goals for this week:

1. ....

2. ....

3. ....

Don't settle for what you already know; always find an avenue to increase your knowledge.

Date	THURSDAY Action Items	Status

Date	FRIDAY Action Items	Status

Date	SATURDAY/SUNDAY Action Items	Status

Today I am grateful for: ....

....

Weekly affirmation: ....

....

WEEKLY OUTLOOK

MONDAY		
Date	Action Items	Status

TUESDAY		
Date	Action Items	Status

WEDNESDAY		
Date	Action Items	Status

Top 3 goals for this week:

1. ....

2. ....

3. ....

Give the present day your full attention and best effort.

THURSDAY			FRIDAY			SATURDAY/SUNDAY		
Date	Action Items	Status	Date	Action Items	Status	Date	Action Items	Status

Today I am grateful for: ....

....

Weekly affirmation: ....

....

# MONTHLY REFLECTION

Take an opportunity to review the month.

Which goals did you complete this month?

....

....

....

What was your favorite moment this month?

....

....

....

Who or what kept you motivated this month?

....

....

....

What is something positive from this month that you can bring into the next month?

....

....

....

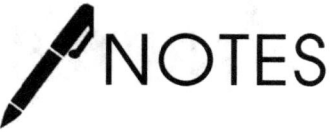 # NOTES

MONTH 9

FOCUS YOUR THINKING

What you deem important directly impacts the trajectory of your success!

MONTHLY DISCOVERY

There is an affirmations page at the beginning of this planner, the purpose of which is to encourage you to focus on yourself and what you're thinking. Your thoughts are extremely important and can impact your daily performance and achievements. Focused thinking is an intentional effort to discover and develop ideas. Sometimes, this is an area that challenges many of us. What you think on a consistent basis often impacts how you live your life. When was the last time you examined your thought process? Have you ever considered something you wanted to accomplish, but before you could explore the full capacity of that thought, several negative thoughts began to creep in? Perhaps these negative thoughts crept up on you with such force that they buried the initial thought, rendering it lifeless before you could even take action.

What you deem important may directly impact the trajectory of your success. In the book *Thinking for a Change*, John C. Maxwell explains, "One reason people don't achieve their dreams is that they desire to change their results without changing their thinking." If you changed your thinking, what kind of impact could you make? Which goals could you accomplish?

Positive thinking optimizes the number of possibilities in your life. This level of thinking invites you to view circumstances from a different perspective. How many goals would you achieve if your thinking changed?

Using Affirmations to Refocus Your Thinking

We can occasionally fall into negative thoughts and self-talk. As a result, these negative thoughts can diminish fulfillment in your personal life, productivity, self-esteem, relationships, and career. One way to offset negative thinking is to use positive affirmations. Positive affirmations are statements used to challenge and overcome negative thoughts. They are mental repetitions that can redefine your thinking—switching your thought process from negative to positive. Affirmations are usually short statements you can use to describe how you would like to see change within yourself or circumstances. You can write down these statements or record them for listening purposes.

Creating Personal Affirmations

You can create and apply affirmation statements to personal circumstances. To create affirmations, first analyze the thoughts or behaviors you'd like to change in your personal and professional life. The best way to start is to review your goals and strategically come up with positive, credible, and achievable affirmation statements that are the opposite of your negative thoughts in that same area. If you find it difficult to create your own affirmations, consider using quotes from a book, identifying your favorite scriptures, or pulling from other text that will support your positive thoughts.

Your goals and the process used to achieve them are necessary to create the changes you would like to see in your life. I intentionally used statements to promote engagement and build confidence within you. Before moving on to the next section, return to the affirmations page and read the statements aloud to yourself.

TAKE ACTION

This month, I challenge you to focus on your positive thinking and create a personal affirmations plan to reengage the same. Take a moment to reflect on positive statements you want to say to yourself. Next, use the space provided to create a positive affirmations plan using statements to balance your negative thoughts and self-talk. Repeat your affirmations several times a day, especially whenever you find yourself slipping into negative self-talk or engaging in negative thinking.

THINK IT OVER

1. What negative thoughts and/or self-talk do you believe are sabotaging your goals?

....
....
....
....

2. How did you react while reading the earlier affirmations aloud to yourself?

....
....
....
....

MONTHLY CALENDAR

SUNDAY	MONDAY	TUESDAY	WEDNESDAY

THURSDAY	FRIDAY	SATURDAY

Monthly Goals

1. ....
2. ....
3. ....
4. ....
5. ....

Friendly Reminders

1. ....
2. ....
3. ....
4. ....
5. ....

WEEKLY OUTLOOK

MONDAY		
Date	Action Items	Status

TUESDAY		
Date	Action Items	Status

WEDNESDAY		
Date	Action Items	Status

Top 3 goals for this week:

1. ....

2. ....

3. ....

Redefine your thinking by changing your perspective.

THURSDAY			FRIDAY			SATURDAY/SUNDAY		
Date	Action Items	Status	Date	Action Items	Status	Date	Action Items	Status

Today I am grateful for: ....

....

Weekly affirmation: ....

....

WEEKLY OUTLOOK

Date	MONDAY Action Items	Status	Date	TUESDAY Action Items	Status	Date	WEDNESDAY Action Items	Status

Top 3 goals for this week:

1. ....

2. ....

3. ....

For as he thinketh in his heart, so is he. —Proverbs 23:7

THURSDAY			FRIDAY			SATURDAY/SUNDAY		
Date	Action Items	Status	Date	Action Items	Status	Date	Action Items	Status

Today I am grateful for: ....

....

Weekly affirmation: ....

....

🔍 WEEKLY OUTLOOK

Date 📅	MONDAY Action Items ✈	Status ✓	Date 📅	TUESDAY Action Items ✈	Status ✓	Date 📅	WEDNESDAY Action Items ✈	Status ✓

Top 3 goals for this week:

1. ....

2. ....

3. ....

Positive thinking optimizes the number of possibilities in your life.

THURSDAY			FRIDAY			SATURDAY/SUNDAY		
Date	Action Items	Status	Date	Action Items	Status	Date	Action Items	Status

Today I am grateful for: ....

....

Weekly affirmation: ....

....

WEEKLY OUTLOOK

MONDAY			TUESDAY			WEDNESDAY		
Date	Action Items	Status	Date	Action Items	Status	Date	Action Items	Status

Top 3 goals for this week:

1. ....

2. ....

3. ....

Take life day by day and learn to focus your thought patterns and move in a positive direction. —Z. Robinson

THURSDAY			FRIDAY			SATURDAY/SUNDAY		
Date	Action Items	Status	Date	Action Items	Status	Date	Action Items	Status

Today I am grateful for: ....

....

Weekly affirmation: ....

....

MONTHLY REFLECTION

Take an opportunity to review the month.

Which goals did you complete this month?

....

....

....

What was your favorite moment this month?

....

....

....

Who or what kept you motivated this month?

....

....

....

What is something positive from this month that you can bring into the next month?

....

....

....

 NOTES

NOTES

MONTH 10

RELEASE YOUR FEARS

I have learned over the years that when one's mind is made up, this diminishes fear; knowing what must be done does away with fear.

—Rosa Parks

MONTHLY DISCOVERY

When was the last time you experienced fear? I'm always amazed how this short, four-letter word can bring a range of emotions to the surface, change an individual's perspective, cause someone to act out of character, and paralyze growth. The ironic thing about fear is that related emotions you experience are sometimes not realistic. Have you experienced the emotions of fear? Which thoughts come to mind? How did you feel?

During my reflection time, I couldn't help but think about the number of times I've experienced fear when attempting to achieve something. However, a driving force from within allowed me to push past the fear and move forward to complete

the task before me with a great sense of accomplishment as well as excitement and relief. It was afterwards that I realized I had almost talked myself out of this accomplishment because the fears behind my emotions and concerns were false.

One example that comes to mind is when I wanted to start my own business. Convinced of the type of business I wished to open, the audience I wanted to serve, and the kind of service I wanted to offer, I made the decision to write my thoughts down on paper and list everything I needed to work on: including a website, social media presence, marketing materials, etc. While creating this list, I began to experience an overwhelming feeling of fear. I stopped to look closer at the situation and began to question my emotions. I later understood that my fear resulted from the decision to step out and do something so courageous without knowing how these efforts would turn out in the end. I am delighted to share that I did not allow fear to stop me, and I in fact did the very same thing I am challenging you to do this month. I chased down my decisions and ran in the direction of my fears. I didn't let uncertainties and "what if" factors play a role in shaping my decision to start a business. I challenged myself to consider the other side of my perspective and decided to see how things would gradually pan out.

Fear activates something within. For some, it is the driving force that makes them push ahead to the next level, but for others, it collides with our thought process and stops movement. Which category do you fall under? If your thoughts around fear are left unchecked, this often leaves you in a stuck or stifled position and steals from you the ability to move forward. It delays your actions and diminishes your sensory desires to try. Our reactions to fear can cause us to feel paralyzed and afraid to challenge ourselves to "do it afraid."

Which fears are blocking you? If you have formed a habit of giving up on your goals due to fears, use the following strategy to combat this problem. Using the acronym R.E.S.E.T., think through the following principles that can help you release your fears:

R – Realize your potential

E – Eliminate excuses

S – Structure your thinking

E – Emerge by developing disciplined actions

T – Trust your inner ability to accomplish a new goal

TAKE ACTION

This month, I would like to challenge you to release your fears. Using the R.E.S.E.T. principles, identify 3 to 5 areas where you would like to do this.

1. ....
2. ....
3. ....
4. ....
5. ....

Apply the R.E.S.E.T. principles to create a strategy for how you will release your identified fears. Write it down here.

....
....
....
....
....
....
....
....
....
....
....
....

THINK IT OVER

Which principle(s) will you commit to applying today?

MONTHLY CALENDAR

SUNDAY	MONDAY	TUESDAY	WEDNESDAY

THURSDAY	FRIDAY	SATURDAY

Monthly Goals

1. ....
2. ....
3. ....
4. ....
5. ....

Friendly Reminders

1. ....
2. ....
3. ....
4. ....
5. ....

🔍 WEEKLY OUTLOOK

Date	MONDAY Action Items	Status

Date	TUESDAY Action Items	Status

Date	WEDNESDAY Action Items	Status

Top 3 goals for this week:

1. ....

2. ....

3. ....

Chase down your decisions and run in the direction of your fears.

THURSDAY			FRIDAY			SATURDAY/SUNDAY		
Date	Action Items	Status	Date	Action Items	Status	Date	Action Items	Status

Today I am grateful for: ....

....

Weekly affirmation: ....

....

WEEKLY OUTLOOK

Date	MONDAY Action Items	Status

Date	TUESDAY Action Items	Status

Date	WEDNESDAY Action Items	Status

Top 3 goals for this week:

1. ....

2. ....

3. ....

The greatest mistake we make is living in constant fear that we will make one. —John C. Maxwell

THURSDAY		
Date	Action Items	Status

FRIDAY		
Date	Action Items	Status

SATURDAY/SUNDAY		
Date	Action Items	Status

Today I am grateful for: ....

....

Weekly affirmation: ....

....

WEEKLY OUTLOOK

Date	MONDAY Action Items	Status	Date	TUESDAY Action Items	Status	Date	WEDNESDAY Action Items	Status

Top 3 goals for this week:

1. ....

2. ....

3. ....

Fear delays your actions and diminishes your sensory desires to try.

THURSDAY			FRIDAY			SATURDAY/SUNDAY		
Date	Action Items	Status	Date	Action Items	Status	Date	Action Items	Status

Today I am grateful for: ......

Weekly affirmation: ......

WEEKLY OUTLOOK

MONDAY			TUESDAY			WEDNESDAY		
Date	Action Items	Status	Date	Action Items	Status	Date	Action Items	Status

Top 3 goals for this week:

1. ....

2. ....

3. ....

Do not allow uncertainties and "what if" factors to play a role in shaping your decisions.

THURSDAY			FRIDAY			SATURDAY/SUNDAY		
Date	Action Items	Status	Date	Action Items	Status	Date	Action Items	Status

Today I am grateful for: ....

....

Weekly affirmation: ....

....

MONTHLY REFLECTION

Take an opportunity to review the month.

Which goals did you complete this month?
....
....
....

What was your favorite moment this month?
....
....
....

Who or what kept you motivated this month?
....
....
....

What is something positive from this month that you can bring into the next month?
....
....
....

NOTES

Month 11

FIND THE RIGHT BALANCE

Balance is essential to your well-being.
One way to achieve this is to intentionally implement habits
that will encourage success in this area.

MONTHLY DISCOVERY

The pressures of life can complicate our daily balance in relation to achieving personal goals. Stresses of life, work, outside activities, and engagements can cause us to lose focus on the importance of balance and what this can mean in our lives.

When was the last time you conducted a personal balance checkup? Every individual is unique, and balance means something different to everyone. However, it is essential to your well-being, and one way to achieve this is to intentionally implement habits that will encourage success in this area.

Maintaining balance is important for reducing stress and avoiding burnout. It helps keep us grounded and prevents us from overloading ourselves in any one endeavor.

To maintain balance, we must create time for activities we need to do alongside those we want to do. Each component is necessary and vital when the goal is to live in peace and harmony. At times, we develop habits wherein we focus on one aspect of life while neglecting another. For example, there was a time when I worked excessively and thus had little or no time to rest. Eventually, I began experiencing moments of exhaustion and knew my body was trying to tell me I was overworked. While recovering from fatigue, I realized the importance of maintaining balance. It is important to take time and recognize when our lives lack this. Focusing intensely on one aspect of life without consideration for balance is unproductive.

TAKE ACTION

This month, I would like you to consider the areas of your life requiring balance. Ponder the acronym C.H.E.C.K.U.P. for 7 suggestions to regain this.

    C – Create opportunities for activities you must do alongside those you want to do

    H – Honestly assess your capacity to handle everything on your schedule

    E – Establish a practice not to perform any task or activity to excess

    C – Carve out time for social relationships (family, friends, volunteer opportunities, community initiatives)

    K – Know your limitations

    U – Unplug to maintain balance in all your pursuits and daily activities

    P – Plan your schedule ahead of time to avoid procrastinating and feeling overwhelmed

THINK IT OVER

Which action(s)/endeavor(s) are you performing to excess?

....

....

....

....

....

How can you apply the C.H.E.C.K.U.P. method to your life?

....

....

....

....

....

NOTES

MONTHLY CALENDAR

SUNDAY	MONDAY	TUESDAY	WEDNESDAY

THURSDAY	FRIDAY	SATURDAY

Monthly Goals

1. ....
2. ....
3. ....
4. ....
5. ....

Friendly Reminders

1. ....
2. ....
3. ....
4. ....
5. ....

WEEKLY OUTLOOK

MONDAY			TUESDAY			WEDNESDAY		
Date	Action Items	Status	Date	Action Items	Status	Date	Action Items	Status

Top 3 goals for this week:

1. ....

2. ....

3. ....

Balance helps us remain grounded and keeps us from overloading ourselves in any one endeavor.

Date	THURSDAY Action Items	Status

Date	FRIDAY Action Items	Status

Date	SATURDAY/SUNDAY Action Items	Status

Today I am grateful for: ....

....

Weekly affirmation: ....

....

WEEKLY OUTLOOK

Date	MONDAY Action Items	Status

Date	TUESDAY Action Items	Status

Date	WEDNESDAY Action Items	Status

Top 3 goals for this week:

1. ....

2. ....

3. ....

Done is better than perfect. —Sheryl Sandberg

THURSDAY			FRIDAY			SATURDAY/SUNDAY		
Date	Action Items	Status	Date	Action Items	Status	Date	Action Items	Status

Today I am grateful for: ....

Weekly affirmation: ....

WEEKLY OUTLOOK

MONDAY			TUESDAY			WEDNESDAY		
Date	Action Items	Status	Date	Action Items	Status	Date	Action Items	Status

Top 3 goals for this week:

1. ....

2. ....

3. ....

Focusing intensely on one aspect of life without consideration for balance is unproductive.

THURSDAY			FRIDAY			SATURDAY/SUNDAY		
Date	Action Items	Status	Date	Action Items	Status	Date	Action Items	Status

Today I am grateful for: ....

....

Weekly affirmation: ....

....

🔍 WEEKLY OUTLOOK

Date	MONDAY Action Items	Status	Date	TUESDAY Action Items	Status	Date	WEDNESDAY Action Items	Status

Top 3 goals for this week:

1. ....

2. ....

3. ....

There is a very fine line between loving life and being greedy for it.
—Maya Angelou

THURSDAY			FRIDAY			SATURDAY/SUNDAY		
Date	Action Items	Status	Date	Action Items	Status	Date	Action Items	Status

Today I am grateful for: ....

....

Weekly affirmation: ....

....

MONTHLY REFLECTION

Take an opportunity to review the month.

Which goals did you complete this month?

....
....
....

What was your favorite moment this month?

....
....
....

Who or what kept you motivated this month?

....
....
....

What is something positive from this month that you can bring into the next month?

....
....
....

NOTES

# NOTES

Month 12

END-OF-YEAR ASSESSMENT

Celebrate the wins in your life!

MONTHLY DISCOVERY

"Making the final touches" is one of my favorite statements! To me, it represents an opportunity to review the work I have accomplished to date. Moreover, it provides an opportunity for me to give something one final review before moving on to the next endeavor.

As we enter the final month of this productivity planner, I want to challenge you to reflect on what you have accomplished to date and identify the steps you need to take to put the final touches on the past year. Did you accomplish your goals? Did you learn something new about yourself? Which strategies worked well this year? What were your growth areas?

TAKE ACTION AND THINK IT OVER

We're combining the "Take Action" and "Think It Over" sections this month, as the primary action should reflect on all accomplishments over the past year..

Carve out some time and put the final touches on your year. Review the completed activities throughout your planner and respond to the following questions:

1. What are you most proud of this year?

2. Where/how did you spend most of your time and energy?

3. What were your most meaningful moments?

4. Which new skills did you learn?

....
....
....
....

5. Who or what had the biggest impact on your life this year?

....
....
....
....

6. What did you let go of?

....
....
....
....

7. In three to five words, how would you describe the past year?

....
....
....
....

 NOTES

MONTHLY CALENDAR

SUNDAY	MONDAY	TUESDAY	WEDNESDAY

THURSDAY	FRIDAY	SATURDAY

Monthly Goals

1. ....
2. ....
3. ....
4. ....
5. ....

Friendly Reminders

1. ....
2. ....
3. ....
4. ....
5. ....

WEEKLY OUTLOOK

Date	MONDAY Action Items	Status	Date	TUESDAY Action Items	Status	Date	WEDNESDAY Action Items	Status

Top 3 goals for this week:

1. ....

2. ....

3. ....

The road to success begins with your effort to step out of your comfort zone.

THURSDAY		
Date	Action Items	Status

FRIDAY		
Date	Action Items	Status

SATURDAY/SUNDAY		
Date	Action Items	Status

Today I am grateful for: ....

....

Weekly affirmation: ....

....

WEEKLY OUTLOOK

MONDAY		
Date	Action Items	Status

TUESDAY		
Date	Action Items	Status

WEDNESDAY		
Date	Action Items	Status

Top 3 goals for this week:

1. ....

2. ....

3. ....

Pause, reflect, let go, renew, and start again!

THURSDAY				FRIDAY				SATURDAY/SUNDAY		
Date	Action Items	Status		Date	Action Items	Status		Date	Action Items	Status

Today I am grateful for: ....

....

Weekly affirmation: ....

....

🔍 WEEKLY OUTLOOK

Date 📅	MONDAY Action Items ✈	Status ✓	Date 📅	TUESDAY Action Items ✈	Status ✓	Date 📅	WEDNESDAY Action Items ✈	Status ✓

Top 3 goals for this week:

1. ....

2. ....

3. ....

Spread love everywhere you go. Let no one ever come to you without leaving happier. —Mother Teresa

THURSDAY		
Date	Action Items	Status

FRIDAY		
Date	Action Items	Status

SATURDAY/SUNDAY		
Date	Action Items	Status

Today I am grateful for: ....

....

Weekly affirmation: ....

....

WEEKLY OUTLOOK

MONDAY		
Date	Action Items	Status

TUESDAY		
Date	Action Items	Status

WEDNESDAY		
Date	Action Items	Status

Top 3 goals for this week:

1. ....

2. ....

3. ....

Approach each day with a new perspective.

THURSDAY			FRIDAY			SATURDAY/SUNDAY		
Date	Action Items	Status	Date	Action Items	Status	Date	Action Items	Status

Today I am grateful for: ....

....

Weekly affirmation: ....

....

MONTHLY REFLECTION

Take an opportunity to review the month.

Which goals did you complete this month?
....
....
....

What was your favorite moment this month?
....
....
....

Who or what kept you motivated this month?
....
....
....

What is something positive from this month that you can bring into the next month?
....
....
....

# NOTES

Is your daily routine ordinary or overwhelming? Are you intentionally setting goals that will move you toward your purpose? Are you looking for an accountability tool that will inspire you to actively set goals, make decisions, and assess your progress? If you have a desire to grow, feel like you have lost your drive and direction, and/or need to unlock your potential, look no further than this productivity planner to refresh your mindset and reignite your why.

Brought to you by executive coach Dr. Blair, *Reignite Your Why: A Personal Guide to Getting Intentional Results* will empower you on your journey toward unlocking your full potential. With sections allowing you to schedule activities, set goals, and reflect on your progress, this unique productivity planner serves as a guided tool to help you live each day with intention and is packed with everything needed to check off tasks, meet deadlines, and track personal wins—all while taking the time to nurture yourself and your dreams. Get ready to experience your best year yet!

Dr. Blair is a highly sought-after speaker, facilitator, and executive coach who enjoys sharing her expertise on various topics at conferences, seminars, workshops, and retreats. As CEO of Strategize for Success, LLC, she strives to inspire leaders to unlock their potential and reignite their why by encouraging innovation, commitment, and passion. Her straightforward nature sparks authentic and energizing conversations that challenge people to identify their inner strengths and abilities, fostering the confidence needed to realize their full potential.

Learn more at www.strategize4success.com

www.ingramcontent.com/pod-product-compliance
Lightning Source LLC
Chambersburg PA
CBHW080747060526
44119CB00072B/169